Relatable Reflections

Poems that you may relate to

Gurdeep Kaur

Copyright © Gurdeep Kaur
All Rights Reserved.

This book has been self-published with all reasonable efforts taken to make the material error-free by the author. No part of this book shall be used, reproduced in any manner whatsoever without written permission from the author, except in the case of brief quotations embodied in critical articles and reviews.

The Author of this book is solely responsible and liable for its content including but not limited to the views, representations, descriptions, statements, information, opinions, and references ["Content"]. The Content of this book shall not constitute or be construed or deemed to reflect the opinion or expression of the Publisher or Editor. Neither the Publisher nor Editor endorse or approve the Content of this book or guarantee the reliability, accuracy, or completeness of the Content published herein and do not make any representations or warranties of any kind, express or implied, including but not limited to the implied warranties of merchantability, fitness for a particular purpose.

The Publisher and Editor shall not be liable whatsoever...

Made with ❤ on the BookLeaf Publishing Platform
www.bookleafpub.in
www.bookleafpub.com

Dedication

Hi,

My name is Gurdeep Kaur. I am an ordinary person, who wants to achieve something great in life. I have always wanted to be a great writer. I want to write great novels like *Jane Eyre* by *Charlotte Brontë* and *Harry Potter* by *J. K. Rowling.* Let us see which way the wind blows.

As far as this collection of poems is concerned, I want to dedicate it to the Almighty God, who has enabled me to wield a pen and write something, no matter how trivial it may be.

I hope the readers find something worthwhile in them.

Thanking you,
Gurdeep Kaur

Preface

Though I am no poet of any established magnitude, I aspire to be one. This collection is a tiny step to fulfil my aspiration.

My attempt may impress or depress you. Nevertheless, I am presenting you an anthology of common experiences we all share. I hope they tickel your fancy and resonate with you.

Acknowledgements

I thank the Almighty God for orchestrating the circumstances that enabled me to take on this writing challenge. His divine guidance and inspiration have been my greatest strength throughout this journey. Without His blessings, completing this project would not have been possible.

1. The Tea-Our Own Chai

The divine manna to greet the people we meet,
Our winters' staple and summers' treat,
Never does it fail to raise the heat,
It's available in varied shades of brown and beige.

With sugar and milk, tea leaves are main,
Or the concoction can be taken simply plain,
Cardamom, fennel, cloves and ginger can also it gain,
With all these ingredients herbal status it attains.

Enjoyed equally by young, old, rich and poor,
It can be consumed at home or outdoor,
Moderately taken, it is safe,
Being a stimulant, it keeps us awake.

But, it should be borne deep in mind,
That tea can cause a problem of a kind,
Acidity and ulcers it may form,
On breaking the tea-taking safety norm.

2. Writer's Block

Clock is running tik-tok, tik-tok,
But, I have struck a writer's block,
I have a mighty mountain to climb,
I must write 21 rhymes in the given time.

My mind is stuffy like a flu-hit nose,
My target is not at all close,
I am going through a weird phase,
I write 20 times, then I erase.

My muse has left me high and dry,
I am almost about to cry,
I always wanted to grow,
But my confidence level was low.

This writing challenge has given me a chance,
Now I have to put my mind into a trance,
Lo and behold! I have had made a move,
Here comes a new poem that I have produced.

3. My God

Blessed i'm, not like in ordinary terms.
i'm blessed like no one.

Abundance and protection i receive in unusual ways.
i'm more fortunate than any other human.

Nobody can be more sufficiently provided,
i have everything under the moon and sun.

Though i don't deserve, He keeps me supplied,
He has always upheld my pride.

The best family i have been given,
i can't be more luck-smitten.

My problems evaporate in no time,
By His divine grace i commit no crime.

He has made me sensitive and sensible,
i can't be more compassionate and compatible.

Still i am an ungrateful chap,
i can't thank enough to pay Him back.

i must be grateful for the bounties He gifts me,
For i am a nobody, yet He keeps me.

Even though i fail to show any gratitude,
He is never angry or rude.

i can't match His mercy and providence,
For His existence i need no evidence.

i should take this moment to say to God,
Please forgive me if i'm a fraud.

Make me good, faithful and right,
Let me forge myself in Your blissful light.

4. That Man

The man had a sugar-coated tongue,
A super spiritual tone and an altruistic vibe.
He said he doesn't need much money to thrive.

I thought he was more than the ordinary--
A genuine person and a compassionate man.
But he, too, belonged to the selfish clan.

I asked him for a little help--a tiny advice, a simple
favour.
He acted rude and displayed uncaring behaviour.

He told me he is an omnist--he believes in all religions,
However, he forgot to observe compassion--a basic
human-disposition.

Now, you must be thinking who he is,
Okay! enough of this mystery,
Let me tell you his history.

I used to take medicine from him as he is a doctor,
His medicine was effective and he acted like a protector.

I took medicine from him like a steadfast devout,
I never asked any question or raised any doubt.

Though people said his medicine was expensive,
I never became apprehensive.

Then, one day due to unforeseen contingency,
I had to leave my city of residency.

I couldn't take his medicine in the flight with me,
New city's pharmacists couldn't understand his
calligraphy.

I sent my father to ask him,
He again wrote some undecipherable graffiti.

Again, the thing was not vivid,
But, he said he didn't have time to give.

Then, I sent him the photo of the medicine,
He just had to approve after watching.

The message is till date unseen,
There are two ticks without the blue tinge.

It hurt me hard like a whip
Can a philanthropist indulge in mammon worship?

Definitely it caused me pain,
I don't know who is to blame.

Am I too gullible to act smart,
Is it my foible or some failing on his part?

5. I am a small kid

I don't like homework, classwork is enough,
I'm a small kid, don't make my life tough.

All I want to do is play, I don't have a study plan.
You must learn good manners, I'm already a gentleman.

Yesterday, I lost my car toy, all your fault!
You couldn't keep my things in my vault.

I watch cartoons that fight and scare,
In my dream, then, I see a nightmare.

When they wake me up with a start,
My mother clings me to her heart.

I'm the apple of my parents' eye,
My grandparents, too, don't let me cry.

Still I'm a little troublemaker,
My acts of mischief irk my neighbour.

I'm allowed to make mistakes and learn,
My upbringing is everybody's concern.

My teacher says I'm well-behaved,
I love her she is my favourite.

I'm the beginning of something great,
All will be proud of the future I create.

6. I want a day to come

I want a day to come,
When there will be no need to run.
I will not remain an escapist,
I will be everything in my playlist.

I want a day to come,
When I will be second to none,
First would be my place,
Nothing will be left to chase.

I want a day to come,
When I will become the best human,
In the service of Lord and His creation,
I would make life a happy situation.

I want a day to come,
When little will become some,
Some will increase to enough,
So that all have every necessary stuff.

I want a day to come,
When all noises will be mum,
There will be only peace,
Music and songs to please.

7. No News is Good News.

I was apprehensive about this world,
Media had turned me into a coward,
I had stopped trusting people,
After watching the news amounting to crime thrillers.

News must be for the sake of news,
Media should be wary of the effect it may produce,
Information and education it must impart,
Truth and veracity should be its essential part.

News shouldn't be sensationalised to make profits,
It shouldn't become a toy, a plaything in politics,
People watch crimes shows for entertainment,
Criminals watch them to improve their talent.

Continuous encounters with such news,
Make us negative and recluse,
We stop believing in the goodness of others,
All start appearing thieves and murderers.

This give rise to fear, stress and apprehension,
People become patients of depression and hypertension,
Skepticism seeps deep into our hearts,
News pierce our soul with deadly darts.

It happened to me also,
I stopped reading newspaper and watching news shows,
News and crime channels to me became a source of
negativity and concern,
I began to doubt people and their every intention.

Then, I got a chance to visit a new place,
There I met many a trustworthy face,
It slowly restored my faith in humanity,
Now, I see a positive change in my personality.

News shouldn't become horror shows,
They shouldn't scare people and cause much ado,
News should be scaled to their true proportions,
And good news should also be reported and made
sensations.

8. Hopes and Wishes

Every night in my bed,
I say to myself,
Get up at 5 a.m.,
O you thickhead.

At every dawn in the same bed,
I switch off the alarm,
I sleep till 7 a.m.,
Under my cosy bedspread.

In breakfast, I have butter and bread,
Before lunch, I gobble up snacks,
In lunch, I am again well fed,
At supper, too, my appetite is not yet dead.

Dinner, hardly, skips my head,
I resolve to eat wisely,
But again I forget,
Food makes me braindead.

Some say I am addicted to food,
Others say I don't have control,
For still others I am a glutton,
I think it's my mood.

I promise myself to be good,
Eat less, healthy and freshly-cooked,
Do some yoga, pranayam and evening walk,
But it always remains a tall talk.

I have a height of 5 feet 2 inches,
My weight is 90 kg,
Now that I am obese,
I must start a healthy regime.

Yesterday I visited a doctor,
Like all he said I need to lose some X factor,
X factor is here not something extraordinary,
It is the 'x'es that I have added to my body.

Now I need to shed four 'x'es from 5xl,
So that I can dwell longer in my mortal shell.

9. Can I be a writer?

Writing is not a mechanical thing,
It should emanate from within.

Am I capable of writing?
I don't know I am just trying.

I want to be true to my craft,
That's why I sometimes make a draft.

Many a time I try to cheat,
I use the internet to take a peek.

But rarely I apply the findings,
I comply with my own bindings.

My readers will decide for me,
Am I sincere or slimy?

10. We Need a Reset.

Little work is going on,
A lot needs to be done,
Life is an ongoing classroom,
There is a plenty to learn.

Why do we while our time away in idle pursuits,
When there is a huge treasure to dig,
World has so much knowledge to impart,
We just need to start.

Phone bound life is disgusting,
Books are rather more interesting,
New places are needed to be explored,
Over time thinking should be matured.

Books can open new avenues,
Educational videos can also be viewed,
What we need is a good mindset,
Only education can bring the desired effect.

11. Mind your own business.

I have a 34 year old friend,
She hasn't yet got married to abide by the trend,
This is why people keep on targeting her,
With their mean taunts and behaviour,
She is fed up of this mental harassment,
Mostly at her gym and work department.

She is well-educated, working and smart,
She knows her life needs a new start,
She is ready to enter the wedlock,
As eager as others to tie the nuptial knot,
But shouldn't there be a suitable match,
This union is not a trivial shot.

Even if she doesn't want to try,
Should she be tortured and tried?
People must be taught to bear in mind,
Mental harrasment is also a crime.

12. Rest is underrated.

Don't exert yourself,
Body and mind need rest,
Even machines break down under stress.

Women who plod round the clock,
Like a bullock of the finest stock,
Have to pay dearly with their health,
Which can't be restored with any wealth.

Therefore, dear women take time to relax,
It's acceptable to be a little slack,
When it comes to preserve strength,
We should go to any length.

Self-care is not a luxury to command,
It's a necessity that a body demands,
If you want to be alive and kicking,
Revive yourselves with deep breathing.

Take time-outs to recline and unwind,

This way your life will be long and fine,
Set alarms to remind you this all the time,
We need a shift in work-rest paradigm.

13. My dream home

I want a cosy home,
Made of brick and stone,
It should be thoroughly blessed,
With peace and daily bread.

Its walls shouldn't have ears,
So that no noise can pierce,
Its roof should be strong,
To protect us from any storm.

It should be in serene surroundings,
With chirping birds and views astounding,
From my window, I want to see the meadow,
With cattle grazing and bellowing in trees' shadow.

Sunrise and sunset will add to the charm,
Some flowers around will not do any harm.
Inside there in my room I will make a library,
To surround myself with many a literary luminary.

House cannot be called a home,
Unless it has all precious people along,
My loved ones will grace my place,
I will add all things to their taste.

You will also be invited,
To receive you I will be very delighted.

14. Fleeting Time

I am in a hurry,
To finish a deadline,
My work is still pending,
I have to make a steep climb.

I have been given an extension,
To complete my assignment,
I am still wrestling with time,
To get ready the consignment.

But these two restless kids,
Don't give me a second to sit,
Today they don't want their staple rice,
The new demand is dosa and french fries.

Now, here I am in the kitchen again,
Boiling potatoes in the saucepan,
Everyday I make a new plan,
To finish the task in the given time span.

These kids make me go berserk,
With their fighting and circus,
It is only when they are sleeping,
I can do some silent reading.

Finally, I have got some respite,
Both the children are sleeping tight,
Now, it's time to write a line or two,
Goodbye, you all, the job is due.

15. The Hungry Crow

A long time ago,
There lived a crow,
He was a pro,
Like his famous bro.

Once he was hungry,
He went to all and sundry,
None gave him food,
It spoiled his mood.

He went to a park,
He had lost his spark,
He was about to faint,
He fell down in paint.

He got a whitewash,
There was no black spot,
People now noticed him,
Because of his white skin.

They started greeting him,
Giving him bread or a thing,
The crow understood the suspense,
He continued the pretense.

It was all age-old stereotype,
That black is inferior to white,
Now that he was fair,
He got respect everywhere.

This mentality needs to be challenged,
All colours are pleasant,
Same is with black and white,
Together they make a beautiful sight.

16. My Brother's Wife

My sister-in-law is a fashionista,
Her wardrobe presents an exciting vista,
Her cupboards are crammed with beauty products,
Her wardrobe is a never ending construct.

Her instagram is also full of makeup videos,
She is very fond of beauty studios,
No sale, offer or discount can escape her eyes,
She always gives new freebies a try.

Her vanity box is like Aladin's magical lamp,
It can produce product of any brand,
More than all the world's glam,
She is obsessed with her buying plans.

She is bold and beautiful,
Still she wants a makeover,
Cosmetics only make her feel confident,
Otherwise she is born chic and radiant.

17. Sin of the Silver Screen

Movies, today, are full of violence,
They glamourise illegal offence,
Protagonist is worse than the villian,
In fighting, killing and violation.

Crime is glamourised,
Glamoured ones give crime a try,
People who watch these flicks,
Without realisation they become sadists.

Domestic violence also rise,
People become desensitise,
They grow immune to others' pain,
Who is to blame?

Because moral stories are good,
They are told in childhood,
They have a benign effect on mind,
That is why holy scriptures were designed.

Books of wisdom ennoble us,
They are incorporated in syllabus,
No violent fiction can be taught in school,
Curriculum is not made by fools.

Stop creating and watching gory content,
Movie makers should have a healthy intent.

18. Weighting Woes

I am hungry,
What to eat?,
There's nothing in the kitchen,
Fridge is also empty.

I took dinner at 6 p.m.
It's now 10 minutes past 10,
It's not recommendable to eat at this time,
As late night eating is a crime.

My cousin is a dietician,
She has given me a diet chart,
I have to follow her instructions,
Or she will break my head and heart.

I am already 100 kilograms,
I have been put on a calorie-restriction programme,
I try to honour the eating plan,
I think I need to visit Japan.

Japanese have low body fat,
I must emulate that,
I'm hugely thrilled,
To have that slim build.

19. If Life were

If life were a vacation,
I would have enjoyed every occasion,
If life were a flight,
I would have been at the greatest height,
If life were a golden evening,
I would have spent it dreaming,
If life were a song,
I would have sung it all the way along.

20. Change is permanent.

Are you the same? Nor do I?
Memories fade away, everything is a lie,
As the day passes, so passes the night,
Moon simmers, but the sun is not that bright.
Flowers bloom the same way, rivers flow the same
course,
Birds fly habitually in the old blue sky,
All appears the same, but why don't I?

21. His Grace and Mercy

This disease, that disease,
Medicines have made me obese,
I am fed up of pills and tablets,
I want rest, peace, and happy sunsets.

I make affirmations,
To attract positive manifestations,
I visualise what I want,
I believe in God's gentle grants.

God is merciful to me,
He listens to my every plea,
He answers all my prayers,
I have a fortunate destiny.

I must thank God every second,
He has made my life pleasant,
I always feel blessed,
He never puts me to test.

By His grace, I'm healed,
I'm cured,
My health has been restored,
Thanks to the Almighty Lord.

www.ingramcontent.com/pod-product-compliance
Lightning Source LLC
Chambersburg PA
CBHW070612160726
48003CB00005B/2229